WHICH ARE THE SAME

ANSWER— THE FIFTH PICTURE IN THE FIRST ROW AND THE THIRD PICTURE IN THE LAST ROW.

Printed and published in Great Britain by D. C. THOMSON & CO., LTD., 185 Fleet Street, London, EC4A 2HS.

ISBN 0-85116-429-3

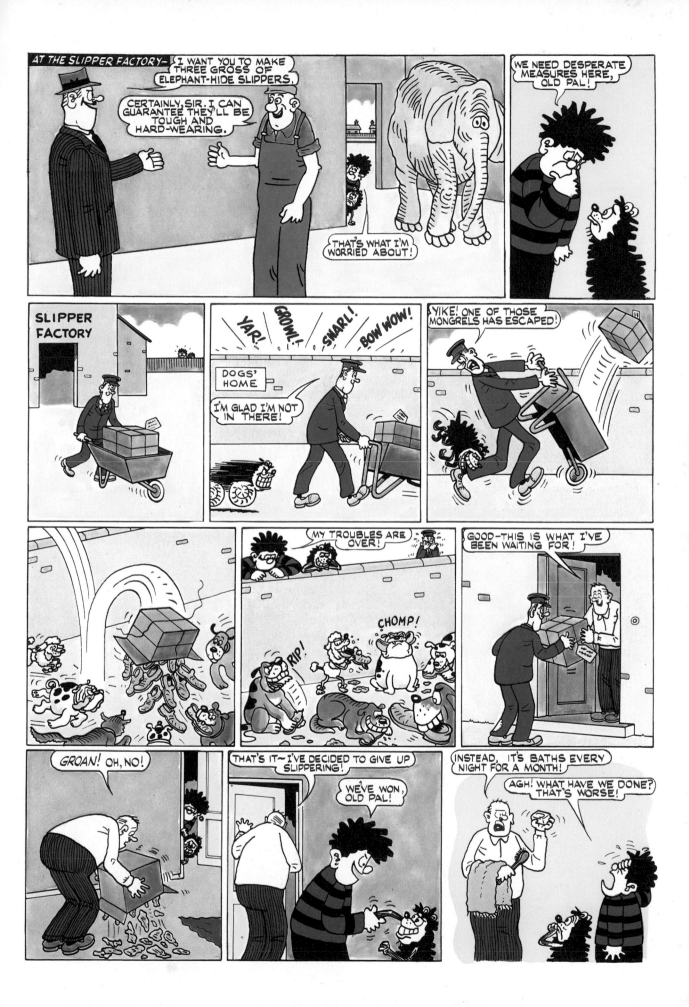

B

HOW MENACING ARE YOU?

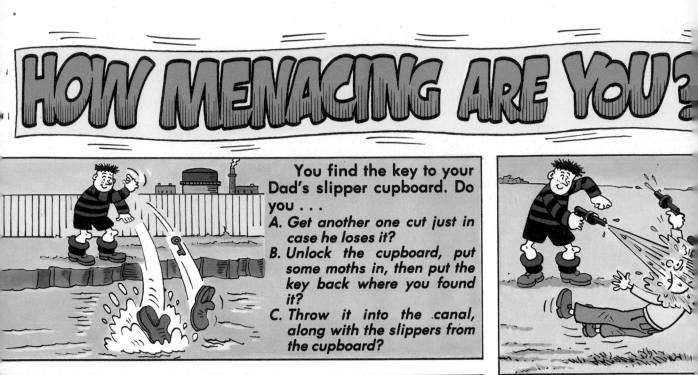

You find the key to your Dad's slipper cupboard. Do you . . .
A. Get another one cut just in case he loses it?
B. Unlock the cupboard, put some moths in, then put the key back where you found it?
C. Throw it into the canal, along with the slippers from the cupboard?

You are not too keen on the new settee your Mum has bought. Do you . . .
A. Embroider flowers on it to make it prettier?
B. Wear a blindfold so you won't have to see it — and have an excuse for "accidentally" spilling things on it?
C. Put on muddy boots and test how good a trampoline it is?

Your dog comes in wi a piece of postman uniform in his teeth. you . . .
A. Offer to sew it back on?
B. Put it with the rest of yo collection?
C. Send him back to chew the rest of the uniform?

Someone asks you if you know the way to the opera house. Do you . . .
A. Tell him the way — and also how simply divine the latest production of Madam Moth is?
B. Give him directions to the wrestling stadium instead — it would be more fun for him?
C. Give him directions to the wrestling stadium and desmonstrate how good it would be?

You are invited to perform with Heavy Metal band, Thunderous Racket. Do you . . .
A. Say "No" — you don't think your delicate lullabies played on the violin would fit in with their loud, nasty noise.
B. Say "No" — you don't think their music is loud, nasty or noisy enough for you.
C. Say "Yes" — and sing so loud and tunelessly you make the band's drummer, Angus "Horrible din" McRiotus, the noisiest man in the world, scream for mercy?

ANSWER THESE TEN QUESTIONS AND FIND OUT HOW MUCH OF A MENACE YOU ARE.....

You are about to squirt someone with your water-pistol, when he makes the "M" for Menace sign. Do you . . .
A. Squirt yourself and run home to Mummykins?
B. Let him off because he's proved his loyalty to Dennis?
C. Squirt him anyway, then have a water-pistol fight?

The "Beano" artist draws you with a Softy haircut. Do you . . .
A. Ask him to add a pony tail at the back?
B. Complain to the Editor?
C. Throw rotten tomatoes at him till he draws you properly?

Your Mum spills some of her best perfume on your jersey. Do you . . .
A. Tell her you want a bottle for your next birthday?
B. Take it off and refuse to wear it again?
C. Rush into the garden to play in the compost heap with your pet pig?

Your Dad wants help changing the oil in his car. Do you . . .
A. Say "No"—you want to keep your hands clean for your embroidery class?
B. Say "Yes" — and get in a super, oil covered mess?
C. Say "Yes" — and take the old oil for your water pistol?

Your teacher tells you your class are going on a nature ramble. Do you . . .
A. Squeak with delight. "I will be able to talk to the little birdie wurdies?"
B. Feel pleased — you love chucking acorns at softies?
C. Feel pleased — you can put on your Tarzan suit and tie up the teacher?

HOW DID YOU ANSWER?

Mostly A — WHAT A WIMP! YOU ARE A REVOLTING SOFTY AND SHOULDN'T EVEN BE READING THIS BOOK! PUT IT DOWN AND LEAVE THE ROOM! YUCK!

Mostly B — YOU ARE A FINE MENACE. YOU OBVIOUSLY READ YOUR "BEANO" REGULARLY AND LEARN FROM IT. YOU WOULD BE A CREDIT TO DENNIS'S FAN CLUB IF YOU ARE NOT ALREADY A MEMBER.

Mostly C — YOU ARE A MENACE AMONG MENACES, YOU CAN ONLY BE . . . DENNIS IN DISGUISE!

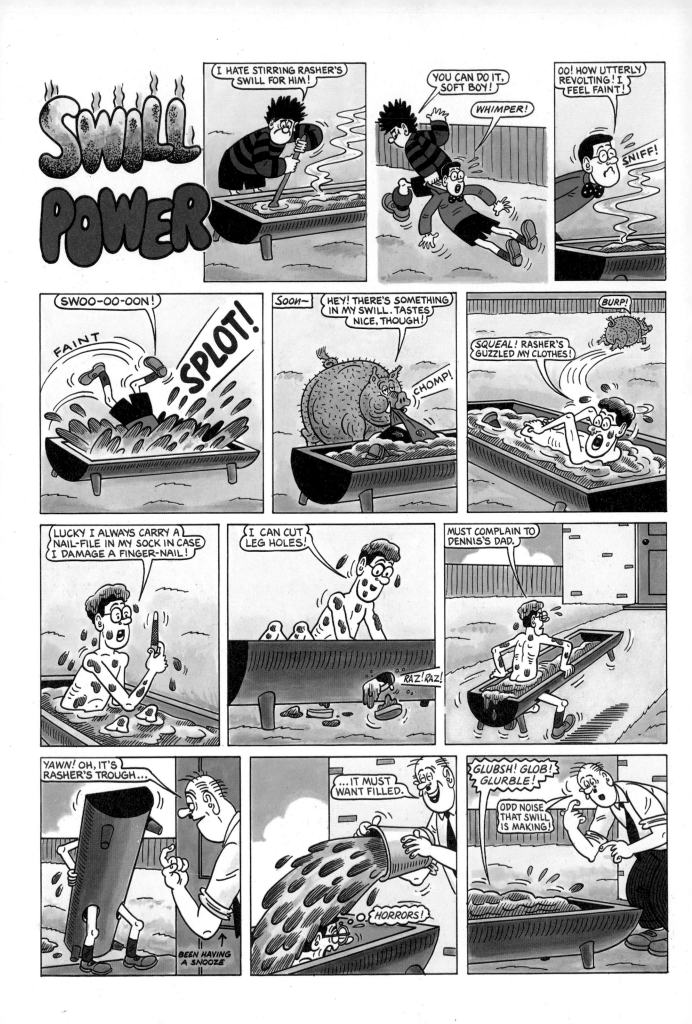

C

RHYMES

This little puppy went to bark at
This bigger doggy with a bone.
That little puppy bit his ankle—
That bigger doggy now has none.
And that bigger doggy went "BOO-HOO-HOO!" all the way home.

Hickory Dickory Dock,
The cat ran up the clock.
The dogs leapt on,
The clock fell down
And gave Mum quite a shock.

"Pussy cat, pussy cat where have you been?"
"I've been to Gnasher's, he's nasty and mean."
"Pussy cat, pussy cat, what did you do there?"
"Dropped lots of missiles from high in the air."

George Porgie pudding and pie
Kissed the girls and made them cry.
When the boys came out to play,
Dennis showed another way.

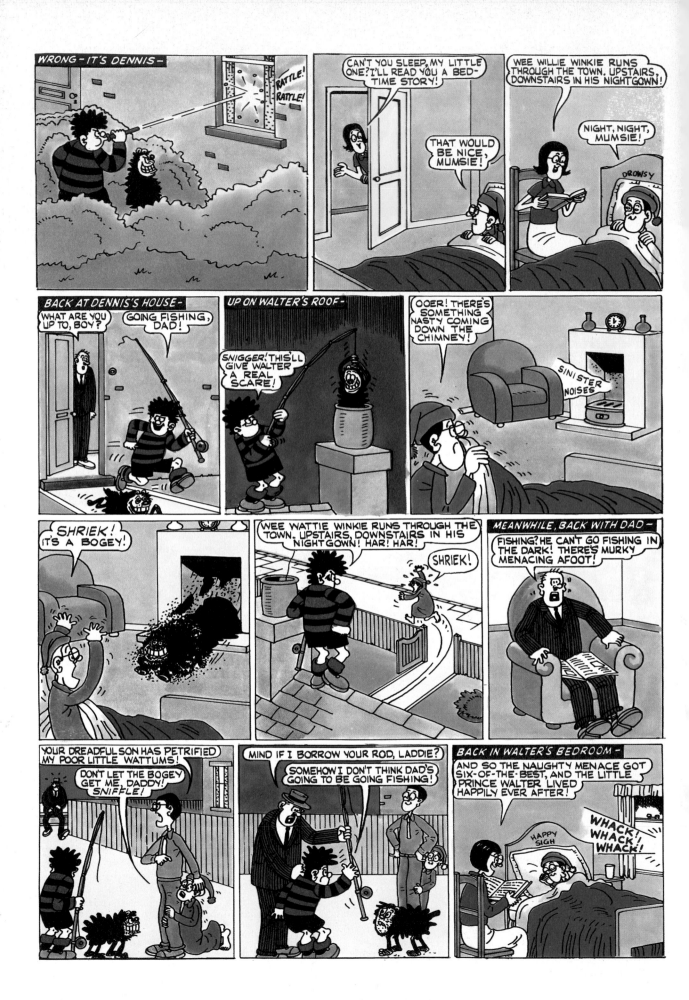

PEASHOOTING STAR

"Slobbering Softies!" yelled Dennis when he saw the telescope at the Beanotown Observatory. "That's the biggest peashooter I've ever seen. Must try it!"

Pausing only to tip a bag of Barlow's Best Peashooter Peas down his throat, he charged in.

"Let me at it!" Before the astronomer (Mr. Venus de Milesaway — he's Greek) could sing "Moon River" backwards — not that he was going to, but you know what I mean — Dennis had his mouth over the end of the telescope.

When all the peas were shot he sighed contentedly — "Ah! I enjoyed that!"

He didn't enjoy what happened next though. The peas hit the lens and shot backwards down the telescope, hitting him in the face. He jumped with rage.

"Who did that?" he looked up the telescope and soon found out. "Wah! It's a Martian!"

"By Jupiter!" exclaimed the astronomer.

"No — by Mars, you fool," said Dennis.

"Actually, near neither," said a small green boy with spiky hair and two wobbly antennae. "I'm from Blurg and I was only sitting on the end of your telescope."

"Save me, Mother!" Yelled Venus de Milesaway, jumping into Dennis's arms.

Dennis dropped him. "Stop it, sap — I'm not your mother anyway." Leaving the astronomer at his feet, Dennis shook hands — "I'm Dennis the Menace, pleased to meet you."

"My name's Zildenbildenbogglebug," said the alien, "but my pals call me Bert, because even they can't pronounce it. I know who you are — we read 'The Beano' on Blurg. Actually that's why I'm here. I came to bring back the paperboy who delivered the last one. Here he is." In walked a wizened old man,

"He's a paperboy?" asked a puzzled Dennis.

"It takes several light years to get to Blurg from Beanotown on a bike," said Bert.

"You can say that again," said the aged paperboy (though no one wanted to say it again) "I was only eight when I left."

Dennis was amazed at what he saw. Hundreds of green people floated about in the air. "Why is everybody green?" he asked.

"Because there's no gravity," said Bert, stepping out of the spaceship followed by Dennis.

Soon Dennis was twisting and turning in the air.

"Wah! This is odd." Then next minute Dennis was green too. "Yurk! All this is making me sick — no wonder you're green."

Before Dennis had time to get really ill, a large man grabbed both him and Bert. "You two are late for school!"

"Oh-oh! It's my teacher," said Bert.

"Where have you been Zildenbildenbogglebug?" asked the teacher angrily, for, being brainy (well as brainy as any teacher is), he knew how to pronounce Bert's real name.

"I've been to Earth to deliver my paperboy," answered Bert.

"Don't be daft — you deliver papers not paperboys — why should I believe you've been to Earth?" demanded the teacher, jumping up and down with rage — and going up a great height since there was no gravity.

"Because I brought an Earthling back," said Bert smugly.

"It's far quicker in my space buggy — want to come?" asked Bert.

"Wild Softies wouldn't stop me!" said Dennis.

So off they went to Blurg. First they went up in the air, turned left at the moon (on which Dennis painted a face) and then headed for the asteroid belt. This had been tightened, so it was a bit of a squeeze gettng through.

Soon Blurg was in sight. It was an odd planet. The top half covered in huge mountains, the bottom half a smooth desert with four huge lakes.

"You can see why you're so famous here on Blurg," said Bert as they zoomed along above the city of New Beanoblurg.

"Ah! If you're an Earthling you can tell me what these odd Earth objects are," said the teacher, pointing to a bike, a double bass and a can of shaving foam.

"Easy — this is a necklace," Dennis said as he placed the bike over the teacher's neck. "And this is a shoe — pity, there's only one," Dennis helpfully told the teacher, as he jammed his feet between the strings of the double bass.

"But what about this?" asked the teacher, holding up the shaving foam.

"Oh, that's something you spray all over your head."

"Why?" said the teacher, his head now completely covered in foam.

"So we can run away without you seeing us," shouted Dennis, as he and Bert floated happily away.

D

Dennis wasn't happy for long, though. "Isn't it about tea-time now?" he asked Bert.

"Yes — and it's my favourite, bouzooki burgers with belchyburp custard, tonight," said Bert, licking his purple lips.

"Yuck! I think I'd better go home," said Dennis turning even more green. "I prefer fish and chips."

"OK" said Bert sadly. "I'll give you a lift."

In no time (well some — but not much) they were over Earth again.

"Cheerio! Thanks for the lift," said Dennis, stepping out of the buggy. Unfortunately he'd forgotten there was gravity on earth and that he was not on the ground.

Luckily he broke his fall by landing in the upturned telescope in Venus de Milesaway's observatory.

Venus was busy showing round some other astronomers.

"And this is the telescope through which I first saw the horrible green man!" he boasted.

"That one?" said Dr. Sputnik, the Russian astronomer, pointing to Dennis who was still looking a bit green — who wouldn't, after falling from a spaceship, down a telescope and into a roomful of astronomers with funny names?

THUMP!

"Grungle grunk glubsh!" he said — remember he was still a bit travel sick.

"That must be his name!" said Dr. Sputnik. "Where do you come from?"

Unfortunately, Dennis was still not in the best of health when he replied. So if you look out your window at night the third planet on the left past the paint spot on the window pane is now called "Groo! Blurgh!"

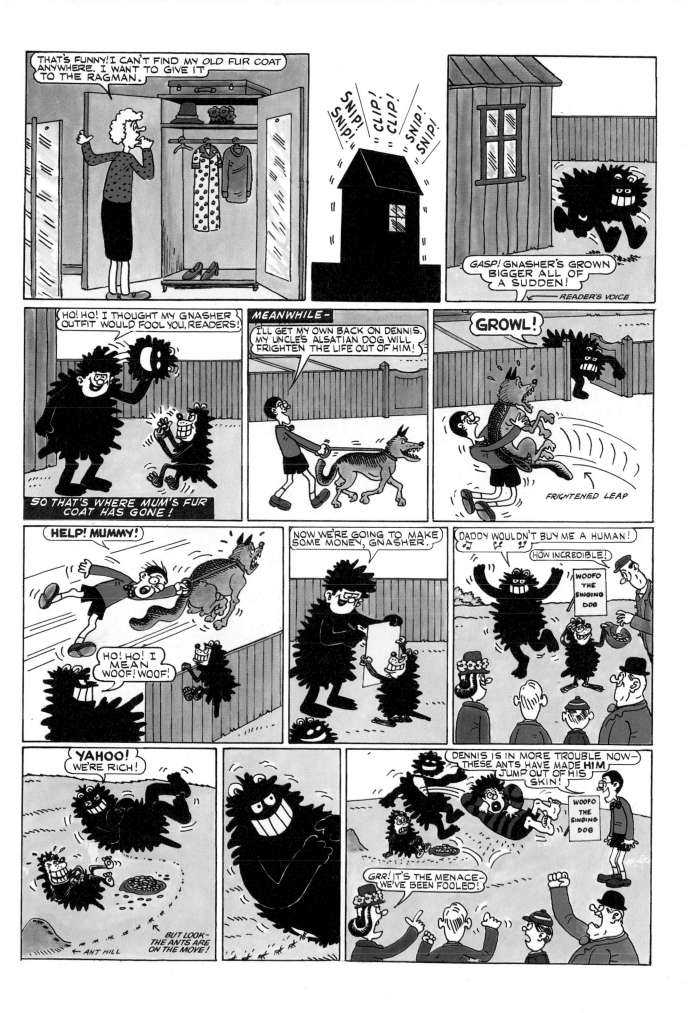

START

ALLOW YOUR OPPONENT TO SQUIRT YOU IN THE FACE WITH A WATER PISTOL.

PRETEND YOU ARE RASHER AND GRUNT YOUR WAY THROUGH "WHITE CHRISTMAS".

DANCE "SWAN LAKE" — AND SINK AT THE END.

S

STAND ON YOUR HEAD AND SAY "BEANO IS BEST".

SAFE

DANCE AROUND THE ROOM SINGING THE WORST SONG YOUR OPPONENT CAN THINK OF.

ALLOW YOUR OPPONENT TO TICKLE YOUR FEET.

To play "Forfeits" each player will need two counters. You will also need a dice, a water pistol, some water, socks, shoes and some coats.

SAFE

PUT ON EVERY COAT IN THE HOUSE.

SAFE

WALK AROUND THE ROOM WITH YOUR LACES TIED TOGETHER.

S

| E | SPEAK WITH AN AUSTRALIAN ACCENT FOR FOUR THROWS OF THE DICE. | SAFE | HANG YOUR SHOES ON YOUR EARS FOR TWO GOES. | SAFE |

This is a game for two Menaces — one pretending to be Gnasher, one pretending to be Dennis. The object is to get right round the board without landing on a forfeit square. Once you have paid your forfeit you must mark the square with your second counter and make a complete circuit from that square to win the game. If you land on another forfeit square you must move your marker and complete your circuit from that one. Gnasher only has to pay forfeits on black squares, Dennis only on red.

BALANCE THE DICE ON THE END OF YOUR NOSE FOR A COUNT OF 10.

SAFE

SAFE

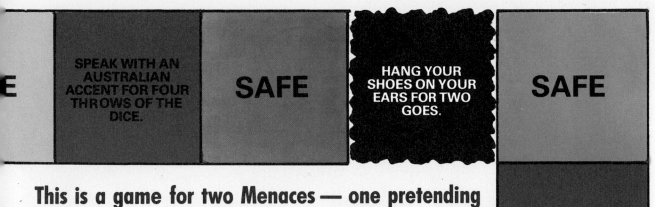

GO OUTSIDE AND SHOUT "I'M A SOFTY".

| E | THROW THE DICE WITH YOUR TOES ON THE NEXT GO. | WEAR YOUR SOCKS ON YOUR HANDS FOR TWO MINUTES. | SAFE | SAFE |

E

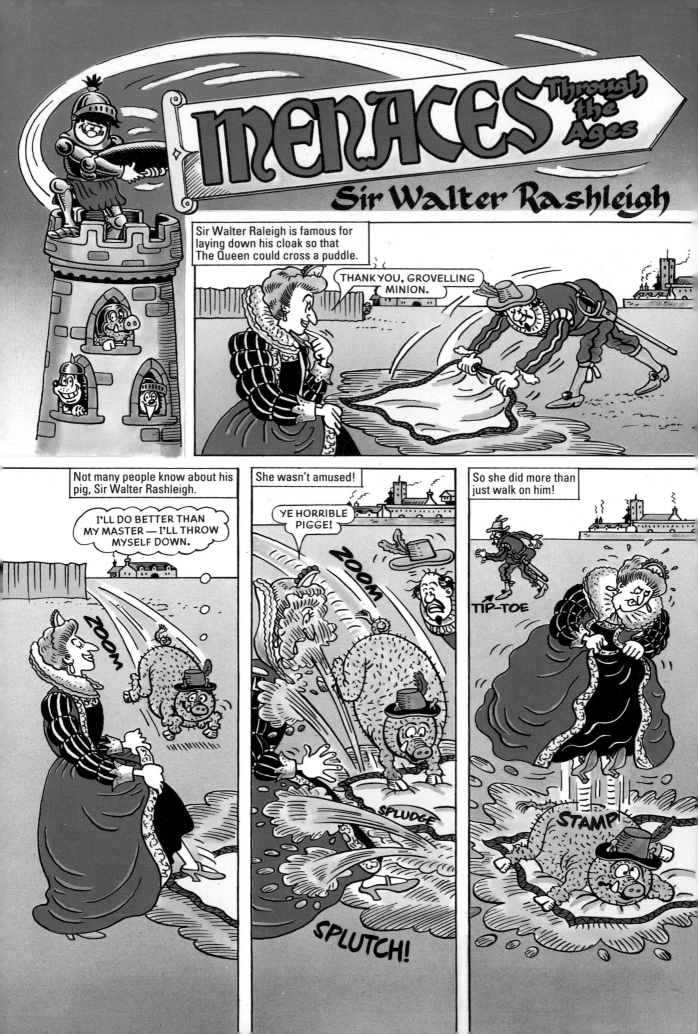

SPOT the BRAWL

IDENTIFY THE OWNERS OF THE THIRTEEN ITEMS INVOLVED IN THIS BATTLE.
(ANSWERS AT FOOT OF PAGE.)

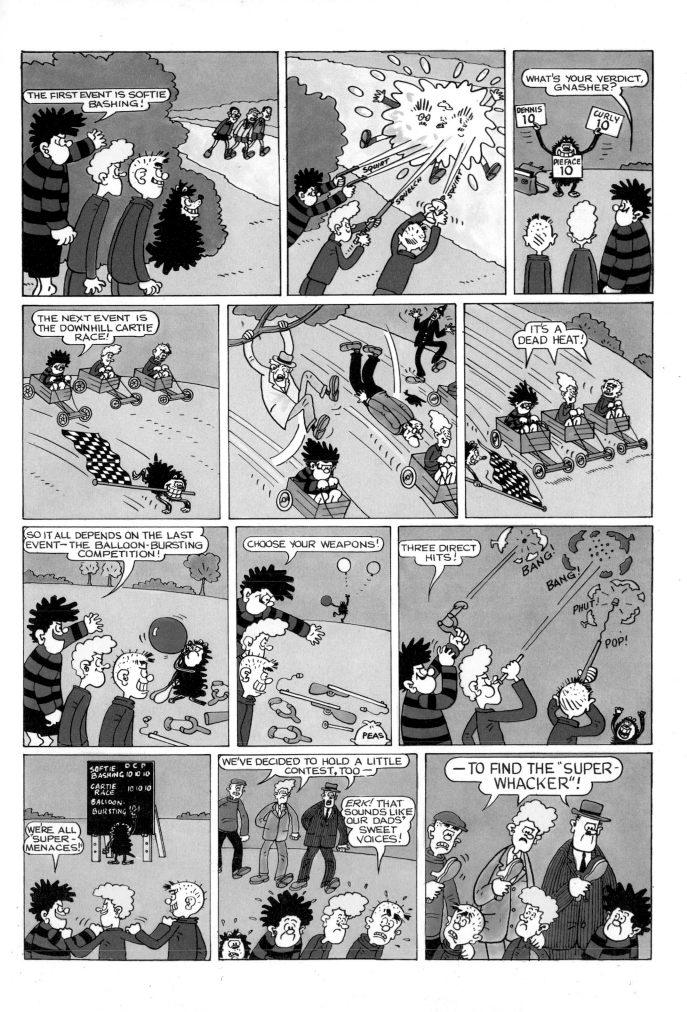

MORE Nursery

Spotty Perkins sat on a wall.
Spotty Perkins gave a loud
  bawl.
Dennis's spiders and Dennis's
  rat
Kept him up there — well,
  fancy that!"

Diddle Diddle Dumpling, my
  son Den
Went to bed with a black felt
  pen.
Drew a face on his bedspread
  then.
Horrid little monster, my son
  Den.

Wring-a-wring-our-
  clotheses,
Dennis found some hoses
Scoosh you! Scoosh you!
All but drowned.

Wee Willie Winkie runs
  through the town
In badly ripped pyjamas
And mangled dressing gown.
Knocking at the windows,
Letting out a wail.
"Gnasher's coming after
  me —
I stood upon his tail."

KNOCK
KNOCK

FLEA FOR ALL

The generals summoned
their armies.
They ordered their troops
to attack.
Foo Foo's fleas wearing a
delicate pink
And Gnasher's a delicate
black.

The D.D.T. guns were soon
blazing.
Insect pellets flew back and
forth too.
The Gnashtroops were very
soon frothing
From direct hits by doggy
shampoo.

In time, when our Gnasher
awakened,
He said, "What's been
going
on here?
My tail is all twisted and
throbbing.
There's elastic attached to
each ear."

"I know who's to blame, it
was Foo Foo."
He said with a fierce
sounding "Gurrr!"
So another fierce battle
soon started,
To resounding "Flea
Cheers!" from his fur.

SPOT THE GNASHER HEA